No

Angela Alston, LADC, LMSW, SAP, AADC

ANGELA ALSTON, LADC, LMSW, SAP, AADC

This is a work of non-fiction. Although some names have been omitted or changed due to privacy considerations; the book is based on factual events from the perspective of Angela Alston.

Cover by: Dan Carsten

Edited by: Chrissy Cutting

ISBN: 172644774X
ISBN-13:9781726447744

NORMAL DYSFUNCTION

DEDICATION

This book is dedicated to my momma, who transitioned from this world on November 25, 2017. She did the best she could with what she had, and she instilled so many great morals in me. I am most grateful for the foundation she laid: to love the Lord. She's not here to see this book come to fruition, but I know she is smiling down from heaven. She was my twin.

CONTENTS

POEM

My world as I knew it…revolved around dysfunction…
Shhh… don't tell keep your mouth shut, so no one can go to jail.

Secrets were my companion, resentments, my best friend, my life
as I knew it was chaotic at its core…

You see… that's why I say… all the more…

Normal Dysfunction.

I managed to live, move and have my being, in pain, hurt, and
despair.
No one would know, that was the plan to act as if…not one would
be aware…

Normal Dysfunction.

Self-hate was my reality, low self-esteem I carried with me…

Normal Dysfunction.

Who would I tell, who would understand the shame, guilt, and the
confusion I felt?

How could there be a God? Who would allow such things for a
child to hear screams, and profanity…?
Beatings…well it was normal for me. My normal, to feel numb,
empty where my heat once dwelt.

Normal Dysfunction.

How did I function in my normality? I did it with a smile, hidden
in deceit. I became an actress, a chameleon, a fake. I couldn't tell

my secrets, I couldn't let anyone know that I became comfortable with…

Normal Dysfunction.

Don't tell, keep the secrets, don't embarrass the family. Even at the cost of me losing my sanity.

All for the sake of saving face, Oh no! I dare not. It was only for His amazing grace. You see I met a man, who showed me my reality that, He had greater plans for me.

That my new companion would be the Holy Spirit that dwelt within me, and would show me a way to Normal… no longer…

Dysfunction.

INVITATION

My name is Angela Alston, and I invite you to read about some of the life experiences that have helped to shape the person I am today. It's my story of dysfunction. It is my hope that you will laugh, maybe you will cry, or maybe you will get angry and decide you will no longer live in dysfunction.

Either way, I encourage you to read these accounts with an open mind. I believe that there are many people that can relate to my story. We may have had different experiences, but we have all come to know "teacher pain" on a first name basis. I understand that everyone may not be at a place of healing, where they can reveal themselves like I have. I shared our story for us.

My hope is that you will no longer stay in bondage but make a decision to start the "journey to wholeness." Change may be difficult and painful but being free is worth it!

I also hope that my story will motivate others to fight their way out of what may appear to be an insurmountable situation.

Whether it's addiction, domestic violence, or holding on to painful secrets.

All things are truly possible with Christ. Even if you don't go to church, don't allow that to be a roadblock. What is most important is: "if you believe it is possible to be healed and set free, then you shall be." However, if you don't believe, then that seed of doubt will manifest. It doesn't matter the seed, what matters most is that it will produce after its own kind. I know that today, healing, joy, and peace are possible; in other words, *All things are possible to him who believes (Mark 9:23).*

ACKNOWLEDGEMENTS

First and foremost, I must acknowledge my Father in heaven, God. I continue to be amazed that He chose me to do this great healing work of the masses. I thank him for healing me, setting me free from bondage, and transforming my life.

I would like to acknowledge my husband: He is my soul mate, my best friend, my biggest supporter, and my confidant. He believes in all of my wild ideas, never questions my ability to achieve my goals, and has supported me through the numerous trials and tribulations I have endured. After 26 years of being together and 19 years of marriage he still makes me giggle like a schoolgirl.

To my Children, you are truly the very best part of me. You were a witness that something good could actually come from me. I love your versatility of personalities, and how each of you are strong in your own unique way. I am amazingly blessed to be your mother. I must say a special thank you to my eldest daughter who gave me the title for this book, your creativity amazes me.

To my siblings, although there's only the 3 of us, we have been through a lot. We accept each other's differences but yet support one another, as Ma would have wanted us to do.

To my family, many of you believed in me from the very beginning and I thank you for that. Thank you for your support, and your love.

T*o my mother-in law,* I don't know how we would have made it without you. You are one of the strongest women I know. I thank you for blessing me with your son. You did a great job.

1 IDENTITY

2 Corinthians 5: 17, "Therefore, if anyone is in Christ, he is a new creation; old things have passed away; behold, all things have become new."

Who am I…? I was born in 1970 in Miami Valley Hospital in Dayton, Ohio. I was conceived outside of marriage and as a result I was led to believe that my sister's father was my father. I understand now but didn't when I was a young child that getting pregnant by someone that was not your husband was not received very well – by the husband or otherwise. My mother later told me that she was embarrassed because she was still married to my sister's father when I was conceived by my "real daddy." It was normal for many of us in our family to find out decades later that the man we believed all those years to be our father was not. I believe that my mother did not want me to feel different, maybe she was ashamed, and I am sure she did not want to hear any criticisms or judgment family. However, she had no idea that the seemingly insignificant omission of truth would have such a great impact on my life for years to come. I remember the day that my cousin told me who my real father was. At that time, my mother avoided the conversation by saying, "she don't know what she talkin' bout…she drunk." It was our family's belief that when somebody got drunk and spilled the beans about a family secret, more than likely they were telling the truth. So when she spilled the beans, I was not surprised because my father had already told me the truth one day when he was babysitting me. I remember he peered around the corner, with a Cheshire cat grin on his face and said, "You know I'm yo daddy right?" In that moment, I felt very special because no matter how dysfunctional the relationship was… "My daddy is here." I thought things would change for sure; I would be the daddy's girl. I had always dreamed of being daddy's girl, but little did I know *the spirit of rejection* had entered in. No one could have known 30 years ago that I would have to battle this spirit for most of my life. What I didn't know is that for

decades I would grow to hate who I was. I hated the color of my
skin, the poverty I was born into, the size and shape of my body,
and my thick, tightly coiled hair that everyone called nappy.
Maybe I would not have listened to the teasing, and the boys
whispering, "I don't wanna play with her because she black and
ugly," or this light skinned guy telling me "you know you kinda
cute to be black!" if someone had instilled in me to love who I was
and that all of my features were beautiful. Maybe just maybe, I
would not have had so much self-hate. It appeared to me that no
one and I mean absolutely no one believed I was pretty. It became
even more evident in fifth grade when I wanted to try out for
cheerleader. My teacher who was fair skinned was in charge of
approving students to try out, and she would not even give me the
opportunity because of how I "looked." She said it was because I
looked mean all the time. I knew it was a lie, but how could I
prove it? I was just a child. In my mind, she didn't want me to be a
cheerleader because she thought I was "black and ugly." This event
was one example of the "Colorism" that I would face for years to

come. The internal message that I was "black and ugly and that no one would ever love me" began to root in my heart. I can recall fantasizing, wishing I was white. In my mind I believed that white people didn't have to go through these things—they had fair skin and were beautiful, they had pretty eyes of all colors, pretty hair that would not get kinky when wet, and they came from families that were not dysfunctional. I believed they had lots of money and sat down at the table together and had meals with their children. All of the things, I didn't have. My only reality was poverty and dysfunction. So even though my perception of what "happiness" was, was unrealistic and distorted in so many ways, anything was better than living the life that I was born in.

2 FEAR

2 Timothy 1:7, For God gave hath not given us the spirit of fear but of power, love and of a sound mind.

As a child I was afraid of: the dark, loud noises, screams, I was afraid to be hungry, afraid of my dreams, and most importantly afraid to disappoint anyone—for *fear* of them rejecting me. The fear started slowly and unnoticeably because I learned very young that I would keep fear my secret. I can remember a particular apartment we lived in Hartford. As I child I didn't know how to explain it, but it always felt "different." I didn't know why at the time, but the atmosphere was different in that apartment. One night as I lay in the bed I could see what appeared to be a man's figure standing in the doorway of our room. It had the build of a man but where the head should have been, it was larger than normal. I blinked my eyes several times to try to convince myself that I was not seeing what I thought I saw. I tried several times, but to no avail; I could still see it standing there. I thought it was moving, coming closer to me. I yelled for my mother. She came in the room in the same doorway that this "thing" was standing, which really confused me because how could she have just walked through the door when it was standing there? At that moment I had to think quick! So, I told my mother that I saw something, but she reassured me that there was nothing there and told me to go back to bed. I still don't know how I was able to go to sleep that night, only by God's grace some kind of way I made it to sleep. Now that I think back on my childhood I was always "special." I don't mean that in a good way either. The kind of special that means I need to be in a special class and see a doctor to be prescribed some medication. This only caused me to isolate more and to keep even more secrets. For example, when I didn't have any homework to do I would lay on the floor with my mother's JC Penny Catalog, flip through all of the sections until I found the jewelry section. At times pages would get stuck, but I would lick my thumb and forefinger; in the way that old men would when trying to loosen dollar bills to give you some money. I was determined to get to that special place. No matter how many times I looked in that book, I never wanted any toys, only a necklace with a crucifix. Of course, I would never tell anyone; it was my secret obsession. I couldn't explain it, and maybe in my immature mind, I thought the cross would keep me safe like in the scary movies. I couldn't explain the internal pull. I was young but old enough to know that people would think I was weird. As I write about these experiences, I can recall my aunt telling me that when I was young, she recalled that her sister-in-law looked at me intently one day and said: "that girl is special she's gonna do great things." My aunt is famous for telling stories. Sometimes we have to follow up with others in the family to determine fact from fiction. However, one story she told me I believed. I was too young to remember this, but deep within me I knew it was true. She said that there was a picture of Jesus Christ hanging in her den. It was one of those pictures with felt material. It reminded me of the old felt picture of dogs sitting at a poker table. I digress, but in the picture, Jesus had blond hair and intense but yet inviting eyes. The story is... one day, she was babysitting me and I walked in the den area; I stopped abruptly and turned toward the picture. She said I stood there transfixed. As I stood there, I began to tremble and cry and no one knew why, or what to do but no one could stop me. What was very clear is that I was in some way connected to the person that was depicted in the picture. This leads me to the day that I could no longer hide my weirdness or what I now know was my connection to the spiritual world. Me, my sister, and our neighbors used to play "church." If you grew up in church, you know what I'm talking about. We would sing church songs, use books to bang back and forth on the palm of our hands to resemble tambourines, and dance around like we had the "Holy Ghost." The only guy of the bunch had to be the preacher. He would preach fake sermons with charisma and full of energy, and we would shout and dance around like we really felt the "spirit." However, things changed on this particular evening. As we were playing church something took over me. That was my first introduction to the Holy Spirit for real. I was crying, and I couldn't stop. Initially no one realized I was serious, then after a while, I could hear them yelling saying, "Ann... what's wrong with you?" I couldn't respond although I wanted to because I didn't want to get in trouble, it was as if something else controlled me. I started getting nervous myself because it was like I was having an out of body experience that I couldn't control. One of my friends ran into the house to get an adult. I remember my father coming outside. By this time, I was able to snap out of this trance I was in, and the tears were still visible on my face. He asked me what was wrong with me, but I lied and told him "nothing." I knew I couldn't explain it to myself so why try to explain it to him? After all, I was afraid of how he would respond. I can recall later that night my friends saying... what's wrong? What happened to you? Once again, no need in trying to explain it because I felt that no one would understand, and it would only reinforce what I already thought about myself. I was always concerned about how others would respond to my unusual experiences. What would people say about me? If that wasn't enough, I began to have terrifying dreams of demons, possessed houses, things, and people. I have had dreams of battling demons in my dreams for as long as I can remember. I never understood them. It's like "here we go again... another weirdo experience" that only caused me to be even more afraid and isolated from everyone else. Although I was terrified every time I had those dreams, my spiritual maturity increased each time. I became more aware of how to fight demons. It's as if the spiritual and the natural worlds were aligning. Initially I did not know how to fight the spiritual entities. I would say childhood prayers in my dreams due to the lack of spiritual growth because I didn't know what else to do. I remember in my first dream reciting a childhood prayer: "As I lay me down to sleep, I pray the Lord my soul to keep, if I should die before I wake, I pray to Lord my soul to take." I find it hilarious now, that prayer was my only weapon. The interesting thing is that I knew to call on the Lord even if it was in a childish prayer I would say before bed. One thing I was sure of, and that is, is I wanted to learn to no longer be afraid. After a while, being scared got very old. As I grew in my relationship with the Lord, so did my power and anointing in the natural and it translated into my dreams. I became a fighter! Finally, I was like yes!!!!! It's on now! I was no longer running from the demons, but I would begin to take the offensive stance and initiate the attack.

One summer, I was in Alabama visiting my family, and my sister and I had to sleep in the same bed that night at my mother's house. In this dream, there was a demon that came to attack me. He was dark, his presence was one of the worst I had ever experienced. He appeared void of any life, but he had a disposition that made me keenly aware that he was there for a purpose and I knew his intentions were evil. At this time, I began praying in my heavenly language "speaking in tongues," and when I began to do that, I began to get more and more energized and less afraid. I began thinking this demon is trying to punk me! Although he was much taller and stronger than me, I gathered all the strength I had and began to run towards it with my right hand outstretched. As I laid my hand on its head, I saw a swirl of what appeared to be a dark funnel cloud, resembling a small tornado coming from the top of his head. At that moment I woke up. As I began to fully wake I had that familiar feeling again. It's almost as if the battle in my dreams always left a residue to ensure I remembered in the morning. I'm not sure how the conversation started later that day, but my sister said that I was jumping around a lot in my sleep, so much so that I woke her up. Until that moment, I never told anyone about my dreams. I finally revealed my secret battles that have plagued me most of my life.

My second encounter with fear was the trauma I experienced because of my father. He not only beat me and my sister with extension cords, but he also beat my mother. He was lucky if he could catch my sister though because she could run fast. Therefore, sometimes, she could escape his wrath. Nonetheless, when it came to my mother, she always "got it!!!" I remember hearing the yelling, he would yell and beat her and talk to her like she was trash. I may have been young, but I knew enough to know that my mother was being hurt and it was because of the only man

I loved. I did not understand why he would hurt her. I remember hearing her cry and scream, and then eventually he would leave afterward. In hindsight, I understand why we moved so much… from Garden Street, to Kent Street, to Sterling Street to Bowles Park. No matter where we moved he would reappear eventually and start beating her all over again. He would cry and tell my mother that he was sorry for his behavior and promised to never to do it again. I didn't know what to think. I was confused because I loved him and wanted to be daddy's girl but each time he was around he would scare me. I eventually developed a nervous problem, which I later learned was anxiety. I'm sure if I had been seen by a professional at that time I would have been diagnosed with several mental health disorders. I can recall an incident in which he beat up his own sister who was visiting from out of town, just because she gave my sister and I toys to play with. These early experiences only deepened my fears and instilled confusion in my impressionable mind about love and relationships.

3 TRAUMA

2 Samuel 22:3, My God, my rock, in whom I take refuge, My shield and the horn of my salvation, my stronghold and my refuge; My savior, You save me from violence.

I have so many different versions of this story in my head. I had to have several conversations with my mother to confirm the accuracy of my memories. I remember it was a sunny day outside, my mother had to go to work and my father was left to babysit me. One version of this story was that I was outside playing and that I had just gotten wet by the fire hydrant, it was our ghetto way of playing in sprinklers. I was laying on the sidewalk to dry off a bit. Shortly thereafter a boy rode by on a bike and I somehow ended up with a huge laceration in my head. Blood was flowing down my face so much so that I could barely see. The second version that I remember: was that I was in the house, I was in my room then suddenly … everything went black. I can recall bleeding from my head and my father telling me that I fell out of the bed and cut my head on the railing. I never knew what really happened that day. I just remember that my head was throbbing, and I was in so much pain. I can recall my mother coming home from work that day, and she was so upset with my father because he didn't take me to the hospital. He just allowed the blood to clot and dry all over my hair. It was difficult for my mother to see the actual injury because the blood was dark red and causing my hair to stick to my scalp. I can recall her asking him what happened. He repeated the same story to her that he told me. She then asked him why he didn't take me to the hospital and he said, "She don't need to go to no hospital; you work at the hospital, you can fix it." After discussing this incident, I asked my mother why she thought he did stuff like that to me and why I would end up with so many mysterious bruises. She regretfully said to me that he told her one day, that he beat me so much because I looked just like her. If that's not enough to traumatize a young child, I don't know what is. I am sure there are several things that happened to me that I cannot remember. One day my sister said to me, "you don't remember nothing?" At that time, I didn't know how to explain it, but I believed God was protecting me to prevent me from losing my mind. The last and most terrifying incident that involved my father happened when I was in the 3rd grade.

My mother believed in her kids doing chores and helping out around the house. It didn't matter how old we were. This night I was standing on a kitchen chair washing dishes. I had on a brown leotard and tan and brown pants that were "high waters." My mother, sister, and newborn brother were in the living room area. We had recently moved into this apartment building for our safety. This building was different from others because in order for someone to get to our third-floor apartment, they had to be buzzed in. So, as I was washing the dishes, I heard the doorbell chime, but I didn't pay much attention to it. My attention was focused on finishing the dishes. I wanted to hurry up and finish so I could resume watching Family Feud with my mother and sister. However, as I was caught up in my own thoughts, I heard something that seemed out of place. I heard my mother scream. Initially, I thought somebody on Family Feud must have just won a prize. I knew it couldn't have been anything serious because my father couldn't get to us unless someone let him in. After all, he was in jail. Nevertheless, as I stood there, I heard another scream; and this time, I decided I would go see what was going on because something seemed eerie about this one. I walked slowly to the living room area... hands dripping with soapsuds; as I walked closer to the living room, I could see that the door to our apartment was open and my father was standing there with a shotgun pointed at my mother. My mother was cradling my newborn brother so tight in her arms, I don't know how he was able to breathe. My mother was screaming and pleading with my father not to shoot her. As I stood there in a daze, I could see my sister suddenly dash past me, to the kitchen and toward the back stairs. My mother yelled to her to call the police at our neighbor's house down on the second floor. Evidently, he became distracted by my sister. He then proceeded to run behind her threatening to shoot her. Yelling at her to come back. I told you earlier my sister was fast, well she was supersonic fast that night. She was in a zone—she did not look back but continued to run as fast as she could down the stairs. She made it down the stairs before he had an opportunity to get within arm's reach. There was so much chaos in that moment. I thank God for my sister that night, she probably saved all of our lives. I stood there transfixed in a zombie-like state with hands dripping, my feet could not move. I can recall my mother running past me, down the front stairs, with my baby brother in her arms. My father then retreated back to the living room area where I stood, still standing there in a terrified daze. I think I was so shocked by the events taking place that I didn't realize everyone left me. My mother was gone, my sister was gone. The only thing that was left was me and Family Feud blaring in the background. At this point, he knew the police would be on their way and his plot to kill my mother and possibly all of us was foiled. He then looked down at me and said, "do you want to go with me?" of course I said yes. He proceeded to lift me with one hand while holding the gun with the other while putting me on his back. As he dashed down the stairs, my chin was bouncing up and down on his back, my arms were wrapped tightly around his neck, with my hands clasped together. We proceeded through the downstairs door, and as we did I felt the cold air hit my face, and at that moment I remembered that I did not have on a coat, socks or shoes. My father proceeded to run down the sidewalk then took a right down Edgewood Street. He continued to run, but then stopped halfway down the street to throw the shotgun in the snow. However, as he continued running I could hear the police sirens blazing, the sounds getting closer and closer. He attempted to turn around and run the opposite way, but another police cruiser was closing in. He finally decided to give up when he realized he could not go any further. The police commanded him to stop running, and he slowly complied with their commands. I am grateful that he didn't try to do anything stupid while also holding me. The officers then put us in the police car. While in the car, my father began to whisper to me and tell me to lie to them about the gun. I eagerly agreed. Although afraid, I did not want to disappoint my father. When we got back to the apartment, the officer pulled me from the back seat to bring me back to my mother. It seemed as if my mind finally caught up with my body because I began to shiver uncontrollably. I was so nervous and cold; it seemed that no amount of clothing or heat could stop me from shivering that night. Then unbelievably my father began to tell them that I wanted to go with him. He said to me, "Tell them… you want to come with me, right?" I shook my head yes. I could not comprehend the magnitude of what was going on. He began to yell, "I didn't have no gun! Ann… tell em… I didn't have no gun." My mother began yelling back at him in the background, "yes, you did … yes, you did." The officers appeared to realize that I would say anything to appease him, so they took my father away and began to question me about the gun. I was asked to go with them in the cruiser to show them exactly where he had disposed of it. To my surprise, I remembered, and they were able to retrieve it, then they proceeded to take him back to jail. This was one of his many trips to the

Department of Correction for domestic violence. My mother explained that she was so shocked that he was there that night, as he had recently been arrested for stabbing a close friend of the family during an altercation at our other apartment. She thought he was still locked up. She had given into a false sense of safety because she thought he had no idea where we had moved. Our strategy was each time he was incarcerated we would make our move to an undisclosed location. I can recall living in several different locations in a short span of time; little did I know it was because my mother was attempting to get away from my father. Unfortunately, she didn't realize that some of her friends were conned into telling him where we moved to. After all, manipulation was one of his best tactics. I think at this point my mother began to realize how dangerous he was. Although she suffered many beatings, this was his first time threatening her with a weapon. We will never know if he planned on killing all of us that night. I am grateful that my mother finally began to accept the fact that my father was intent on causing serious harm to us. If we stayed in Connecticut, there was a huge possibility that we wouldn't be as fortunate the next time. I didn't know it at the time, but my father was a heroin addict, which may have only added to his erratic behavior. With that being said, the next move was out of the state to Birmingham, Alabama.

4 DOWN SOUTH

Proverbs 3:5-6, Trust in the Lord with all thine heart, lean not unto thine own understanding, in all thy ways acknowledge Him and He shall direct thy path.

After the incident, my mother gave us the news that we would be moving to Alabama. My sister and I were actually happy because we loved the idea of being in Alabama with all of our family. What we didn't know at the time was that my mother was not coming with us. She planned to stay in Connecticut to sell all our belongings. Therefore, she sent us on the plane with our older cousin. That was the last I saw of Connecticut for the next 10 years, and honestly, I didn't miss it for a very long time. Living in Alabama was interesting. Although, I loved the respect that children had for their elders, and the tight-knit family gatherings, I didn't understand why black folks focused so much on skin color and hair texture. As I slowly adjusted to the Southern culture, I quickly realized that there were some words that kids were not permitted to say. I knew it was bad to use profanity. However, I didn't know that saying that someone told a "lie" was bad until one day my aunt scolded me when she heard me use the three-letter bad word. I didn't know what I did wrong. I had no idea what she was talking about. Later my cousin explained to me that "'lie' is a bad word, you have to say, 'telling a story.'" It's funny now, but it wasn't at the time.

Adjusting to the seasons was very challenging. I also had to adapt to living with a lot of people, considering we didn't have our own apartment. A bunch of us cousins had to sleep together due to us being so overcrowded. We would use a bunch of clothes to cover ourselves with so we wouldn't feel the rats running on top of us at night. I can recall we were so poor at times we didn't have towels to dry off with. Me and my younger cousins would stand in front of the heater after we took a "wash up" to dry off. Just for clarity, a wash up is taking a bird bath at the sink. We would dry off by rotating in a rhythmic fashion. I guess it became a game to us. At times, we would run out of deodorant. Usually, someone would be given the task of throwing a lifeline to our other cousins to bring deodorant in the car. In this way, we could quickly dab on some "Tussy deodorant" before we made it to school. There were days, however, that I didn't have deodorant and when I was in close proximity to my classmates; in the lunch line, I think they were also aware. Someone would yell out "ooohhweee somebody musty!" I would clinch my arms tight to my side while holding my lunch tray, as if that would prevent the stench from escaping from my armpits. It was so embarrassing. It wasn't all bad though. I remember when my older cousin would get her food stamps. I would be so happy because I loved to eat, especially boiled eggs. During the first of the month, we ate well. I loved it. However, the food wouldn't last long and sometimes the rats would get to the cereal before we had an opportunity to open the box. Those rats were just disrespectful, but as long as there was enough left for us, that's all I cared about. I could recall the rats being so bold that when someone stomped their foot to scare them away, they only looked at us and finished doing whatever they were doing. On occasion, they would get too close for comfort. Let me explain.

Sometimes the toilet wouldn't work properly; and in order for it to flush, you would have to manually flush it by pouring a bucket of water in it. Unfortunately, there were times when you just had to do what you had to do. When this happened, it was very important that when you used the bathroom that you look in the toilet first. We never knew when one of our playmates would be swimming around in there. We actually named one of the rats "My Nig"—he would be hanging out in the toilet sometimes.

We couldn't afford air conditioners, so we had to place the square fan in the window to blow the same dry heat that was outside, inside. I quickly learned to spend a lot of time in the neighborhood swimming pool once we moved to another area with my other aunt. One of the things I didn't realize was that my already chocolate skin would get even darker, as a result of spending so much time in the pool. So, this brings me back to my complexion.

According to the Oxford Dictionary, the definition of Colorism is "prejudice or discrimination against someone with a dark skin tone, typically by people along the same racial or ethnic group." If you can recall at the beginning of this book, I spoke about how I wished I was white or light skinned. This is why. I was already insecure, traumatized, had low self-esteem, and thought I was ugly because I didn't have pretty hair. Now I had to deal with this from my other people. It's not that people in my family would call me ugly. It's just that they had a weird way of making you think you were beautiful. I used to ask my mother if she went through that and she said she didn't. She said she never had an issue with how she looked. Which made sense, why she didn't notice the insecurities in me. The way this worked was, if you were light skinned, you were the best thing since sliced cheese. But if you were dark skinned, forget it! I often would hear… "oh you're kinda cute" or "you kinda cute to be black." I would attempt to bleach my skin, using bleaching cream to see if I could get lighter. Of course it didn't work, and it only served to increase my insecurities and feelings of rejection. As a result, I constantly focused on how ugly and nappy headed I was and listened to my self-talk about how no one would ever want to "go with me." As a result, my sense of self-hate slowly began to grow. The traumatizing experiences with my father, the lack of a positive man in my life, and this growing self-hate began to develop into a cascading flow of bad choices.

As a teen, I grew up in the projects, which we called LVP. I can recall the day, my sister and I realized that everyone that lived in the projects was cussing. I remember when my sister and I were on the side of the house and she asked me... "Ann, we gonna cuss?" Before you knew it, we became very proficient at using profanity. There was a sense of community in the projects, we played outside until the street lights came on. Eventually our mothers would begin to call us to come in. We had gym parties, we raced in the streets, we went to the only Summer camp that we had access to "Ms. Betty B. bus," and we played tackle football. We frequently would have competitions over who had the "livest" front. If I we were going to tell it, Garfield Lane was the best. We were poor, we had roaches, oh boy did we have roaches. We had so many roaches that when the exterminator would spray, the floors and cabinets would be littered with roaches of all sizes. I hated that time of year because the combination of dead roaches, the awful smell, and the sound of roaches crunching under my feet would cause me to lose my appetite. The roaches were disrespectful as well. If you were foolish enough to put your glass of Kool-Aid on the floor, roaches would be backstroking in it by the time you picked it up again. We were so poor, we had to borrow sugar, bread, and sometimes put a meal together by borrowing several items from several different people. Regardless of our poverty, we had so much fun. We had a little store called "The Stand." It was extremely small, and it was so hot in that little box that you felt like you could sweat out your perm. If you had "natural" hair at that time, forget it! However, it was the closest store, we had access to without a car. The store's owner had a visual disability, so if you were the lucky one that was ordered to go to the store to buy your mother's tampons, you already knew to prepare for embarrassment. She would hold them up, really close to her eyes to confirm she had the right brand and size. We would buy microwaved cheeseburgers, pickled pig feet, penny candies, dill pickles, and "goodies" when someone suffered from a hangover. It was fun while it lasted, but unfortunately, she had to close the store. The numerous break-ins seemed to outweigh the benefits of remaining in business. Once the store closed many "candy ladies" began to emerge in the projects. The candy lady was no one in particular just an individual who recognized entrepreneurial opportunities. They would sell everything from candy apples, pickled pig's feet, pickles, and beebops to penny candies. Everyone had to have some type of side hustle in order to make ends meet if they lived in the projects. Our next-door neighbor did hair. She gave me a Jheri curl. The smell of the products was horrendous, but you couldn't tell me I wasn't cute. I had "good hair" now. Her husband sold fish on Fridays or chili dogs and French fries. Others made accessories like socks, barrettes for children's hair or braided hair for a reasonable fee. We had the most fun at our community gym. This is where we would have the best parties and sometimes get free lunch. Those were the best memories. However, as I began to grow into a young woman, many of the traumas and insecurities began to heighten in the same place that I had so many wonderful memories.

Our house was considered the party house. My mother, her cousins, and her friends (that we nicknamed "the untouchables") were frequently at our place, playing Spades and partying. I witnessed a lot of things that just became a part of my "normal." For example, one night, I came back in the house to find out my cousin's husband got shot in our kitchen. He survived the shooting, but the most amazing part was, the aforementioned group of people were in the kitchen playing cards. I was told that a verbal altercation ensued and shortly thereafter gunfire ensued. I can't imagine the scene at that moment, but nevertheless, no one called the police. For some reason—maybe it was shock, or maybe he was just drunk—he ran from the kitchen, up the stairs, turned right into our room and eventually jumped out of the window to escape. Only to leave a trail of blood behind all over our clothes, the closet, and the floors. No big deal. We just preceded to salvage as much of our clothing as we could. We never were able to remove all the blood from the walls though.

As I grew into my teenage years, my mother dated, and at times, two of her boyfriends lived with us. I can recall not having much of an issue with her dating, but I did have an issue with them living with us. I didn't understand why she would allow men to stay with us, considering we were maturing, going through puberty, and trying to find ourselves. I didn't trust anyone because of the trauma I had already experienced with my father. Therefore, it was extremely difficult for me to live with men. I must have known something was coming.

One of my mother's boyfriends my sister and I nicknamed "Chester…Chester child molester." Trust me, he lived up to his nickname. One day when I came home from school, he was in the kitchen cooking spaghetti. After I said hi, he asked me if I would go to the stand to get a jar of spaghetti sauce. I told him I would go, but I would be right back. When I came back in the kitchen to get the money, he said to me: "you know Ann, you look good." I responded, "thank...you." I didn't know what else to say, or what this was leading too, but then in the next breath he said, "you know we should go out sometime." I was dumbfounded. I said to him, "what you talkin' bout? You go with my mother." He said, "she don't have to know nothing." I began to think really fast because no one else was home. I started feeling creeped out. I said, "let me go the spaghetti sauce and I'll talk to you when I get back." I got out of the kitchen so fast, ran outside, slamming the screen door shut behind me. As you might have guessed, we didn't have spaghetti that day. I did not come back home until he was gone. Although I was initially afraid of how my mother would respond, I decided to tell her anyway. I said to her that I have to tell her something. I recounted everything that happened. She said, "Ann... you tellin' me the truth?" I said, "yeah Ma, you know I wouldn't lie about nothing like that." I could see the betrayal and pain all over her face. I am so grateful that I told her because he was kicked out immediately. I felt bad for her and thought that would probably prevent her from having anyone else live with us. I was wrong.

A little while later, my mother met this guy. I thought he was funny looking and didn't understand what she saw in him, but I know my momma. He had what I called the typical "wet mouth look." In today's vernacular, I would say he looked like he was an alcoholic. I guess it didn't matter, he must have given her whatever she wanted, because that was the only reason in my mind that she would have been with him. She eventually married him. As we got to know him, he seemed like a nice guy. However, we liked him the most when he was drunk. We knew we could use his car and he would give us money when he was drunk. We didn't have any issues with him being intoxicated; after all, we were used to people hanging around our house that drank. He was a functioning alcoholic. He went to work every day and gave us money, so we accepted him.

On Fridays, we would go to his job to get money because we knew he got paid. There were nights he would come home and go straight up the stairs, and in a moment's time, we would hear loud thumps. We would run upstairs only to see him sprawled out on the floor. Many times he hit the floor really hard, but he would fall fast asleep where he laid. The next day I would see him and ask him what happened to his face, and he would say, "Well, baby girl, my face got into a fight with the sidewalk." I thought it was funny, but in my own way I felt sorry for him. He was the type of person that when he wasn't drinking (which was rare), he was quiet and didn't bother anyone. However, when he was drunk, he changed. I can recall one night I had my boyfriend over and he happened to come home to catch us in a compromising situation. After my boyfriend left the house that night, I was so afraid he was going to tell my mother and I think he knew that. As I came back to the kitchen after walking my boyfriend to the door, he said, "I know you scared I'm gonna tell you momma, but I won't tell her if you let me see something." Immediately I had a sinking feeling in my stomach. It was late at night and everyone was asleep, I didn't know how desperate I was, but I would find out momentarily. He went on to say, he wouldn't tell my mother, if I would only show him what I let my boyfriend see. I stood there frozen in fear, trying to think as fast as I could, how this situation could possibly play out. I figured, he's not trying to touch me so I will let him see my breast. So, I hesitantly lifted up my shirt and quickly pulled it back down. I guess that wasn't enough because he said I had to do it again. I did it again, but this time he reached out to touch me. He proceeded to touch my breast until I finally moved away and told him to stop. At that moment, I could care less if he told. I didn't think about it at that moment, but if he would have told, then I would have told, and he would have been in the worst predicament. Nevertheless, I didn't tell. I kept that secret, never telling anyone for a very, very long time.

I didn't know it at that time, but my stepdad was molesting me. I was never familiar with the term. All I knew was that he was a "nasty man." I began to develop a better understanding of what "nasty men" were really quick. As I mentioned previously, my house was the place where everyone hung out to have fun. There was always some type of excitement going on in the projects.

Well, with the excitement came a lot of other stuff. For example,

at times people would hang out at our place until late night or

sometimes spending the night. One of my relatives was married to

a guy who began hanging over our house a lot. After all, our house

was the hot spot. My sister and I always thought of him as a little

weird. It's like we knew he was creepy, but no one ever talked

about the "pink elephant" in the room until years later. There were

times when I would go to sleep and wake up the next day feeling

funny "down there." I felt as if someone had touched me. I didn't

know what was going on until one night I happened to wake up

only to find "Mr. Creep man" standing in my room. He quickly

ran out, so fast in fact that he bumped his head on the side of the

wall. After that day, I smartened up and started sleeping in layers

of clothing. I would be very hot and uncomfortable, but I knew if

he tried to touch me, I would wake up before he had the

opportunity to finish. I can't recall how many times he molested

me, all I know is I hated him for a very long time. I found out later that my sister and other relatives had similar experiences. My sister was smart, she slept with a box cutter under her pillow—she would "cut ya." I wished I was a bold as she was. Being molested early in life only added to the trauma I had already faced. Which only compounded the level of dysfunction that was a part of my everyday existence.

5 DYSFUNCTIONAL RELATIONSHIPS

*Psalm 34:15, The Lord is close to the brokenhearted and saves
those who are crushed in spirit.*

It was my eighth-grade year. My friends who lived next door
had a cousin who I thought was so handsome. I knew he was older
than me, but I didn't know by how much. Honestly, I didn't care.
I was still a virgin and was trying to act "grown." I began to go
over my friend's house more and more, just so I could get glimpses
of him. I didn't really know how to act; I was only 15 and never
really had a "real boyfriend." I started asking my friend about him,
where he lived, if he had a girlfriend, all the good stuff. Finally,
she must have told him that I liked him because he approached me
one day and started a conversation. He lived in another housing
project with his mother and his siblings, but he decided to live with
his aunt, who was my next-door neighbor. We continued to talk,
on a daily basis. I learned more about him, so I thought, and I told

him everything I had been through in my life up until that point. I met what I believed to be my "first love." He had a golden-brown complexion, was handsome, was in great shape, he dressed really nice, always smelled good and was "bo-legged." Now if all those attributes weren't enough, having a boyfriend that was "bo-legged" was like hitting the lottery. In hindsight, I felt like I hit the jackpot. I was the luckiest girl in the world because he also had a job. By all fairytale standards, he was my knight in shining armor. I was so flattered that an older guy would like me; I didn't care that it was illegal for me him to be with me. I was 15, and he was 20 years old. I wanted to be sure that I would keep him and prove to him that he chose the right one. I would be everything he needed me to be. I had no idea what I was getting myself into. I remember when my mother first met him she asked me how old he was. I purposely lied about his age. Even though our age difference was considered statutory rape, it didn't matter to me—I was in love. Initially, our relationship was awesome! He gave me money; he brought me lingerie, clothing; we took professional pictures together; he introduced me to all his friends, his family; he took me out to eat at restaurants; and he introduced me to drugs and alcohol.

I felt like an adult, I felt like this guy really did love me. I felt I like a princess, but I still couldn't believe that he wanted to be with me, "this black girl, with nappy hair." I felt like a million bucks, but that only lasted for a little while. Eventually, I started noticing that when my boyfriend drank alcohol, he would get angry over the smallest things. I brushed it off because, after all, nobody is perfect, and other than his slight change in demeanor when drinking he was a pretty good guy. Also, I figured, he wouldn't have gotten angry if I would have done whatever it was he asked me to do. I was willing to do whatever I needed to do to keep him happy. I didn't need for anything, he treated me like I was his wife. I thought, if this is what it means to be married then I'm all for it, I love this man. However, slowly we began to have verbal altercations, and I would say all manner of things to him, and his response was terrible. We would go back and forth yelling at each other, and then eventually make up. Initially, I thought it was cute. Nevertheless, approximately a year into the relationship (when I was 16 years old) he hit me for the first time. I don't remember why, but I do remember that I had never been hit so hard in my life, it felt like fire! I did not know how to respond. As I stood there holding the side of my face, he began to cry and apologize profusely for what he had done; while begging me to forgive him and telling me that he would never do it again. I didn't realize it at the time, but it was the same thing my father used to say to my mother. Then I remembered my mom saying, "if you get hit one time, he will hit you again, and don't you believe him when he say he won't do it again!" Now that I was in an emotionally and physically abusive relationship, I felt embarrassed and ashamed. I couldn't tell anyone, especially my mother, considering what I saw her go through. He was cheating on me as well. Some cases I found out about by someone telling me or by me taking a trip to the free clinic because he had given me another disease. I can recall each time I took a trip to the clinic, I would pray that I wouldn't get the same lady. I was so embarrassed at this point. I was embarrassed, but I didn't do anything to change it until my last visit. During this visit, she performed the necessary test only to confirm what I already knew. He had given me another disease. She looked at me and said, "what are you doing to yourself? If you keep getting these diseases, you won't be able to have kids when you grow up." Although I walked away with another prescription for the familiar yellow and black capsules of penicillin, I knew I had to do something different. Of course, when I would confront him he would lie and say he didn't give me a disease, but we both knew what the deal was, but I stayed anyway.

By this time, he had isolated me from many of my friends and family. He berated me, would tell me I was nothing, and I would never be anything just like my mother. He talked to me like I was a dog. He said things to me that made me cringe. He began to beat me more frequently. I got more clever about how to lie about the bruises on my face. He got more clever as to where he would hit me, as to not leave visible bruises where others would see. My friends were afraid for me; they kept begging me to leave him, but they didn't understand. How could I leave him? He was the first person I had sex with, he was the first man that treated me special, he purchased all of my clothing, and above all… he told me that he loved me. I was confused because I felt as if he did love me. But then again, what was my working definition of love? The only example of a relationship I had was my father and my mother. I believed that love means, you do something wrong you get beat, if you don't do anything wrong, everything will be fine. Nevertheless, the abuse worsened. Regretfully, I didn't want this one opportunity of love to be snatched away because he beat me sometimes. I didn't want to leave. After all, what if what he told me was true and I could never find someone that loved me? I decided to take a risk. I would be very careful not to make him mad, I would do whatever he told me to do, I would wear what he told me to wear and perform sexual acts in the way he told me to. Well, no matter what I did, the beatings continued to worsen over time. So much so that one day we were standing in my kitchen and he raised his hand, and I literally flinched thinking he was about to hit me, when he was just scratching his head. I remember he laughed at me that day. It was as if he knew he had me. I was terrified of him. You see that was the issue with me. I allowed him to abuse me because I thought he loved me and I loved him. I couldn't hurt someone I loved. No matter how much they hurt me.

It was very apparent that he didn't feel the same way because there came a beating that was not only one of the worse but the most embarrassing because, this time, he did it in front of everyone. It happened one night when my girlfriends and I were having a sorority party. I had already told my boyfriend the location so that he could meet me there after work. I ensured that I stood outside waiting for him because I didn't want him to think that I was trying to be with the other guys. As I was standing outside, I could see his car in the distance. He had a white car, but the hood of the car was off. So, it was easy for me to recognize his vehicle. I stood there waiting as he pulled up to the curb while my friends were on the porch. He parked the car and suddenly jumped and proceeded to swing on me with all his might. He connected with every swing. I was dumbfounded. I was so confused because I couldn't understand why he was hitting me. I didn't do anything wrong. He beat me terribly that night, so much so I thought I was going to die. I had on a white shirt that night, but when I looked down my shirt was covered in blood, it was now pink, with clots of blood speckled throughout. I could hear my friends yelling from a distance telling him to leave me alone. He actually threatened to shoot into the crowd. I guess my friends were really afraid for me at this point; because, before I knew it, my mother's husband arrived. He had his shotgun. I begged and pleaded for him to let us go. I tried to convince him that I was OK and to not make the situation any worse. I know everyone looked at me like I was really crazy. Maybe I was just delusional, but I got in the car with my boyfriend and drove away into the night. The beatings didn't stop. He beat me some more later; I don't remember too much more from that night.

With that being said, eventually I got tired of the beatings, tired of being afraid, tired of him cheating on me, so I started cheating on him. It was close to the end of our relationship. I started dating this guy I met in school. I thought he was cute and he seemed interested, but the relationship was nothing special. He was a friend of my best friend's boyfriend. It was a relationship of convenience. He had a girlfriend and I knew it, but it didn't matter. We were both cheating. This went on for some time and I believe my boyfriend began to think something was going on, but for the most part, I was able to keep our fling a secret. That was, until one day, someone who knew of my infidelity decided she would tell my boyfriend I was cheating on him. I can't recall her rationale, but I can recall being so angry at her, thinking she should have stayed out of my business. I knew this was gonna be a special type of beating this night.

That night was another one of the worst beatings I experienced. I forget how it happened, but me, my best friend, her boyfriend, and the guy I was seeing were all at this person's house we will call "Tattletale" for the sake of my story. I was not aware that Tattletale had set me up. She told my boyfriend we were there and called him to come over. When my boyfriend arrived, I was terrified. I couldn't believe my eyes. I was inside "Tattletale's" house, and my boyfriend kept telling me to come outside he wanted to talk to me. I eventually went outside because he kept telling me he wasn't going to do anything to me. He even told me he would bring me back over there. Finally, he asked me, "Who you want? Just tell me and I will leave you alone." I told him I didn't want either of them. My friend that I was cheating with later said, had I said him, he would have broken up with his girlfriend to be with me, but I never believed that. I thought I was making the best decision to prevent getting the crap beat out of me. Well, I don't think that tactic really worked because once he convinced me to get in the car with him, I knew I was in trouble. I don't know why I thought he wouldn't hit me. He used a different tactic this time. He didn't take me in the house, he took me to the side of the house. Our apartments were made of brick. I don't know what I was thinking, but I remember he threw me up against the brick wall and I fell to the ground with a thud, which was when he began to stomp me several times in my chest, all I could do was lay there and try to protect myself by balling up in a fetal position; I was lucky to survive that beating.

Not long after this event, I knew that this would not work. I was either going to end up severely hurt, or possibly killed. I continued seeing the other guy, but I had not quite broken if off with my boyfriend yet. My best friend and I decided that one night we would go spend time with her boyfriend and his friend. She was living with us at the time, so it made it easier for her and I to make up stories as to why we needed to use my mom's car. This night was initially not any different from any other. Except that, as we were on our way back home from visiting our men, my boyfriend seemingly appeared out of nowhere, like in the scary movies! He was speeding, waving frantically at us telling us to pull over. I screamed, telling my best friend to keep driving and to drive faster. He continued to chase after us until he was able to pull his car in front of us, screeching to a halt, blocking our path. He jumped out of his car, yelling and screaming at us telling me to get out of the car. I thank God my best friend was driving that night because she was better skilled than I was. She was able to back up quickly and drive around his car. He jumped back in his car and continued to chase us down the street. We knew we would not make it to our house, so we stopped at "Tattletale's" house to call my mother. Tattletale lived in the back of the projects, so my mother was not pleased to know she had to walk over there to get her car. This was the night, I finally told my mother everything. The police were called, I gave my boyfriend his stuff back, and a restraining order was put in place. He was told he couldn't be within a certain distance of my school, my job or near my family's house. It took me some time to get over him. I did eventually, but the damage had been done.

One might think that I learned from that experience and would never end up in another abusive relationship. Well, I guess I had not learned my lesson yet. I thought the next guy would be different. I thought he would respect me and treat me the way I deserved to be treated. Unfortunately, that was not the case. I met him one day while I was at Majorette practice at my high school. He appeared to be pretty enamored with me, I was flattered, so I spoke with him after practice. He was smiling so hard and telling me how pretty I was. I wasn't going to talk to him, but he was so sweet he wanted to walk me home. He actually held my books for me. That old familiar feeling began to arise. I recall thinking, I'm gonna take it slow, no need to rush into anything. At this time, unfortunately, I didn't know what it meant to take things slow. I jumped from one relationship to the next, never healing from the past hurt. So, this one was no different. Except that this guy was a special kind of crazy. He would do stuff like come and pick me up and give me a ride to school in a stolen car. I should have known better, but I guess I didn't. I found out later what happened because there were several cars stolen from a dealership and it was all over the news. He eventually got caught and had to spend some time in juvenile detention. I can recall writing to him and, of course, expressing how much I loved him, and he would do the same. I had no idea how crazy he was until he showed up at my front door one day. I knew he was supposed to be locked up, so I was shocked. I asked him if they let him out, and why he had that big cut on his arm. He later explained that he escaped from juvenile and while doing so he got caught on the barbed wire fence. Eventually, I began to think something was wrong with him. I also found out later that he was obsessed with sex. He would make me do so many crazy things, and he would get very angry if I wouldn't do them. He would also hold me hostage at his grandmother's house by taking my mother's car; therefore, forcing me to stay at his house. I was so angry at myself. I couldn't believe I found myself in the same predicament. Soon the beatings started. I did learn something from the first relationship because I didn't stay in this one long. When he arrived at my door one day to show me enthusiastically the letter A he branded on his arm, I knew he was "special." I made up my mind soon after that to leave him. I can recall the conversation we had, in which he was threatening me, telling me how bad he was going to beat me the next time he saw me. Finally, the words came from my mouth "you and what f@#a*&nG army?" I had practice that day and he knew where it was located. I went to practice although I was afraid. I rode my moped and carried my box cutter with me. He never showed up. I was so nervous I could barely remember my routines. I realized that the moment I showed him I wasn't afraid, he left me alone. I am grateful that I made it out without too many physical scars, but I definitely had my share of mental ones. Unfortunately, one of the girlfriends he had after me wasn't that lucky. He killed her. I knew God was protecting me once again.

After this failed relationship, I lost all respect for myself. I dated guys that I knew only wanted a sexual relationship. I would spend money on them that I gained from unsavory means. I became very promiscuous at this time. It was no longer about having a relationship. It was all about being in control. I used my body to control men. It was as if, I had a vendetta against them. I didn't care about anyone's feelings least of all my own. I was very calculating. However, there came a day that changed my life.

One day I went over one of my friend's house; we had a "friends with benefits" kind of deal. Every time I went over his house, we would proceed to go to his room and do "our thang" but this day was different. We had just finished, and he excused himself and said he would be right back. I laid there for a while not thinking much about it. I could hear voices in the other room, but I didn't recall seeing anyone when I came in; so, I figured that someone must have come over and he was going to get rid of the person. To my surprise, this guy walks into the room that I did not know. I started calling for my friend, but he didn't answer. The guy said, "oh... he ain't coming." I found out later that they had worked out this deal that he could have sex with me. I remember looking around trying to think if there was anything I could hit him with. There was nothing, and before I knew it he was on top of me. He told me if I did what he wanted, he wasn't going to hurt me. I initially tried to resist, but then thought against it. He raped me. This guy really raped me! I remember he just got up when he was finished and didn't say one word but just walked away. I lay there for what seemed like an eternity. I was so scared to move. I didn't know if the guy would still be out there. Finally, after listening to determine if I could hear any voices, I got up as fast as I could and grabbed whatever undergarments I could locate, threw on my shorts and shirt, and ran out of the house. I went next door to his cousin's house. I was frantic! I told her what happened. She knew who the person was that did this to me and eventually her cousin came over there and told her what happened. I was crying and screaming saying that I was going to call the police, but my friend begged me not to. He told me he would get into trouble if his mother found out something like that happened in her house. Eventually, I gave up. I decided against calling the police. I snatched my panties from him, ran into the bathroom, put them on as fast as I could, and ran out of that house.

I jumped on my moped and rode off at a speed that in hindsight could have caused me to crash. At the time, a crash would have felt better than what I was feeling at that moment. We never spoke about it again after that day and I was never the same.

6 BROKEN

Psalm 147:3 He heals the brokenhearted and binds up their wounds.

As you might have guessed, the issues that I endured from childhood to a young woman produced a very broken person. By the time I was 18 years old I had been in several unhealthy relationships. So much so that I no longer cared about myself. The promiscuity only increased after I was raped. It only added to the turmoil because I never told anyone. I definitely was not going to tell my mother. How was I going to explain why I was there in the first place? It was complicated. By that time, I was so broken that I attempted suicide by swallowing a bunch of pills. The only thing that happened was a bad stomachache. At the time, I think it was more attention-seeking than trying to die. I'm grateful today that I didn't succeed. I couldn't imagine what my death would have done to my mother. I was so unhappy. I hated myself, I had low self-worth, I was angry and selfish, and I had low self-esteem. I was so reckless with my mouth, I didn't care if I said something that offended someone; I would be ready to fight if they felt like they wanted to "jump." I allowed guys to use me in every way possible. I was numb. I couldn't feel anything anymore physically or emotionally. I couldn't tell anyone though. I couldn't bear the embarrassment and shame of telling someone what was really going on. I believed people would blame me, ask me how I could be so stupid, and ask the other inevitable question, "why would you allow someone to abuse you sexually, mentally, and physically?" The truth is, I could not have answered them. My mind (will, intellect, and emotions) was all screwed up. I couldn't think straight. I literally hated my existence. I was in so much pain that looking at myself in the mirror was a feat. One thing that came out of this, though, was the ability to present a lie to the world, while inside I was a broken little girl. All I wanted was to be with a man who would love me and accept me for who I was, including all of my baggage. I wanted all of these things, but I had no idea how to obtain them. I wanted love, but I didn't know what love was. I was lost, broken, and mean as a rattlesnake. Anyone that dared come near me, or tried to befriend me, I made it very clear that I didn't want to be bothered. People would say, "Why you look so mean? It ain't that bad, is it?" Of course, I would respond with a sarcastic remark, or I probably cussed them out. What they didn't know was that my "mean mug" had become my defense mechanism. It became the weapon I used to ensure that people stayed away. Little did I know God had other plans in store for me. Restoration was on its way.

7 NORMAL

Romans 8:28, And we know that all things work together for good for them who love God and are the called according to His purpose. 2nd Corinthians 5:17, This means that if anyone who belongs to Christ has become a new person. The old life is gone; a new life has begun.

At the age of 19, my cousins and I decided to move to Connecticut. It was their first time going to Connecticut, but I was returning home. It was bittersweet. Bitter because of the old memories of abuse and trauma and sweet because I was older, on my own, and ready to start over. It was not easy living with other people. I realized I had to grow up very quickly, the vacation was over and real life had clicked in. I realized that it was very expensive to be an adult. Especially an adult with heavy mental and emotional baggage. Although I was in a new state, I continued with the same practices. I began looking for love in all the wrong places, i.e., the club. I met this guy one night, he was cute, we started dancing and next thing you know we were a couple. I didn't know much about him, but I fell head over heels in love with him. He was living a life that consisted of "getting money by any means necessary," and I was OK with that. I was used to guys who sold drugs or robbed people as a means of gaining income. As a result of this, he was arrested early on in our relationship. Soon after he was released, I found out I was pregnant. What I failed to mention was that we barely knew each other when I found out I was pregnant. Slowly but surely, infidelity reared its ugly head again. I began going through the same things all over again in a different state. There were nights when he wouldn't come home. Then I would walk from our apartment to the block to see if he was coming back home and to give him the key. I should have known better. I chased him. I practically begged him to come back to me. He showed me clearly that he didn't want me, but I pursued him anyway. We continued on in this relationship until shortly after I gave birth to my daughter. After I gave birth, my perspective on life changed. It was as if I got stronger, wiser and developed a sense of resiliency I didn't know I had. So much so that I was no longer going to tolerate abuse, cheating or being treated less than what I deserved. He was not the father he needed to be. He would tell my daughter he was going to come pick her up and he wouldn't show. Although she was young, her disappointment was evident. Even though I didn't think much of him, I would never deny him seeing his daughter. Eventually I didn't have to because he ended up going to prison again, this time for 20 years.

At this point in life, I had a job as a teller at the bank. I focused on working and taking care of my daughter. I became acutely aware that I didn't know how to speak appropriately in a professional setting. I was so accustomed to speaking slang along with a "country drawl"; I never learned how to enunciate words and talk properly. I was so embarrassed that I didn't know how to talk, that I would ignore the phone ringing. I knew something had to change. As a result, I would listen intently to the other tellers' conversations, so that I could learn how to speak properly.

I struggled raising my daughter on my own. I didn't make enough money, there were times I didn't have food to eat. If it wasn't for my neighbor who babysat her at the time; I don't know what I would have done. I was grateful that as she got older she only liked rice and oatmeal so it made it very easy to make sure she ate. The other struggle was not having transportation. There were cold winter days, in which I had to wrap her in a comforter and walk to my destination. My legs would be frozen by the time I got off the bus. After work, I would repeat the same thing. Somedays I risked our safety by taking a ride with strangers. I would cry, my tears would be frozen to my face. I would tell my daughter… "mommy gonna get a car one day and we won't have to go through this no more". The cold winters in Connecticut will do that to you.

At this time, I didn't care to date. For the first time since I had hit puberty, I didn't "NEED" to be in a relationship. For the first time, I didn't need someone to be in my bed at night. While I was working at another bank some years later, when I noticed this handsome brown-skinned guy, about 6'1, wearing all black, and Timberland boots walk into the bank. I followed him with my eyes from the entrance, through the ropes, and eventually to being the next person in line. I can recall thinking... "gosh he walks really slow." I guess that didn't really matter to me because I started rushing the other customers… "Can I help the next person in line please!" just so I could get him to my window. Finally, it was his turn. While handling his transaction, I struck up a conversation with him. Eventually, I would see him in the bank every week on Friday. One day, I said to him, "are you gonna ask me for my number?" We began to date shortly thereafter. He was so amazing, I thought "this is too good to be true." I couldn't believe that he was really interested in me, but not only me, he would ask me how my daughter was doing every time we talked. He had a job, a savings account, and didn't have any children. I was so in awe that God would bring me the perfect man for me. He was everything I needed. Eventually, we made a commitment to one another. Not long after, I was pregnant with our child. I knew he would be an amazing father because of how he treated my daughter. Shortly after giving birth to my middle child, I found that I was happy in my relationship, but I still wasn't happy with my life. I still had struggles in my mind, but I didn't know why.

By this time, my cousins had found a church home. Soon after the death of one of my closest friends in Alabama I thought that maybe, just maybe, going to church would help me.

I remember telling my cousins one day that I wanted to join their church. They didn't believe me initially and I could understand why. I had to borrow clothes from them because I had nothing that was appropriate to wear. This is where my life changed. Once I started going to church, I could sense a deep change in me. I had a desire to live different—I wanted to stop doing the things I was doing. I wanted to see if God was real, like it said in the Bible. Interestingly enough, I began to grow quite fast in my spiritual walk. I had many wonderful leaders and spiritual teachers—all of whom taught me how to grow on my own and in my relationship with Christ. I was the Sunday school teacher in my first church, my third church I was licensed as an Evangelist, the fourth church I joined was Bread of Life Deliverance Ministries. I was eventually ordained Pastor and became the Pastor of that church for 3 years. God began healing in a variety of ways. Sometimes through poetry, and others by sheer deliverance. I didn't realize how damaged I was. It took years to restore me. Then more years to mature me. Then even more years to break spiritual soul ties and generational curses. During this time, I began to bring my children to church with me. I began to grow in my relationship with my boyfriend, and I noticed that my thinking about many things in life began to change. I began to have a desire to be married and live right in the eyes of God. We were engaged for 7 years. Finally, we got married on May 30, 1998. I found out I was pregnant with our son a year later. I began thinking about pursuing higher education, which was something I had never thought about before. I began to think on a new level. A new level which included: being whole, having joy, peace, happiness, love, and the fruits of the spirit. No one couldn't tell me that God wasn't real.

I give all the credit and honor to Him that I maintained my sanity throughout all of the hurt, trauma, and pain. I believe that He protected me and gave me favor. Which prevented me from getting caught breaking the law, which could have led to me serving prison time. He protected me from the people that abused me, and he even protected me from myself when I attempted to take my own life. Shame and guilt were the culprits that kept me quiet, and in bondage for most of my life; they became a part of my dysfunction. Today, I refuse to stay in bondage; I am no longer ashamed. I know now that life is worth living.

Which brings me to why I wrote this book. The purpose of this book is twofold. First, I believe that there are many people that can relate to my story. We may have had different experiences, but we have all come to know "teacher pain" on first name basis. I understand that everyone may not be at the place of healing where they can reveal themselves like I have. I shared our story for us. My hope is that you will no longer stay in bondage but make a decision to start the "journey to wholeness." The journey will be painful indeed, which is why it took me so long to write my story. There were times that recounting these experience became too much to bare, so I stopped writing. Although this process was difficult, and the painful memories made me feel incapable of going further, I reached out to a friend/sister of mine who is also an author, and she said, "It's OK, put it down and come back to it when you are ready, and it will flow." I did just as she said, and it worked.

Second reason was that I wanted to show others that you can make it out of what may appear to be an insurmountable situation. All things are truly possible with Christ. Even if you don't go to church or you are not a Christian, don't allow that to be a roadblock. What is most important, which I hope someone can glean from this book is: "if you believe it is possible to be healed and set free, then you shall be"; however, if you don't believe, then

that seed of doubt will manifest. It doesn't matter the seed, what

matters most is that it will manifest after its own kind. Today I

know that healing is possible, joy is possible, peace is possible. In

other words; *All things are possible to them that believe*

(Philippians 4:13).

AUTHORS NOTE

As a Therapist, Counselor, and Spiritual Leader; I have been

afforded the opportunity to listen to the stories of many people;

from various socioeconomic statuses, ethnicities and lifestyles. Yet

one thing remains certain. A person can guilt, or shame themselves

into remaining in a situation. At times one may believe that it is

easier to stay. Or they may justify the condition and tell themselves

that it is not that bad. The reality is, anytime that a person, lives in

contradiction to their higher selves, he or she will find it very

difficult, if not impossible to be happy.

Another reason why so many people can't seem to find true

happiness is fear. It may seem illogical but fear has prevented so many people from living their best lives. Fear can be healthy in an appropriate way. However, if it prevents an individual from changing for the better, reaching positive goals or spiritual growth it is not healthy. The reality is that those who may be afraid to make difficult changes, are also challenged with thoughts like: "I won't be accepted anymore", "people will think I'm weak", "they may think I'm stupid", or "what if I fail again". I would challenge those ideas with "what if you never found out what was on the other side of fear?"

Please understand, I am very much aware that it is "easier said than done". Therefore, the lens in which I am viewing this from is one of compassion and empathy. Nevertheless, I implore you to challenge your fears. Are they based on reality? Or are they based on "what if". Once you determine the root of your fears.,

dig in, pull those roots up, and start fresh. What is the worst that can happen? I believe the worst that can happen is: stagnation, unhappiness, anxiety, depression, and merely existing. Life is too short.

I have learned this from personal experience. As I mentioned in the dedication, my mother suddenly passed away on November 25, 2017. I can recall my husband waking me up at 3 o'clock in the morning, with a devastated look on his face. The room was dark, but with a slight glimpse of illumination from the television. I could see clearly that he was crying. He said "Bae, it's your mother. I said…"what do you mean, it's my mother?" He said, she's gone. I said, what you mean, she's gone? He then repeated what he said and informed me my brother was trying to call me.

At that moment, I had never experienced that level of fear and dread. I can remember jumping out of the bed, picking up my phone and calling my brother. As soon as I heard him on the other end of the phone crying, I knew it was real. I have never seen or heard my brother cry. Slowly reality set in. I realized that it was true. Although, many of the events shortly thereafter were a blur; I could recall throwing on anything I could find, while getting a bag ready. I don't know where I thought I was going but I did it anyway. I asked my husband to bring me to my sister's house.

It seemed as if time stood still. All I could do is walk around in the yard mumbling to myself…"this don't make no sense!", "this don't make no sense!". At that moment I wanted God to make sense of my pain, and the uncertainty. I wanted instant comfort, but I received none. I could not think of any scriptures to quote to make me feel better. The only emotion I felt was fear. The darkest, unbearable, gut wrenching kind. While at the same time, I instantly began to wail and cry because I wanted to see my momma. Needless, to say, that couldn't happen. I was in Connecticut and she was in Alabama. In that moment for the first time, I experienced a sense of hopelessness and powerlessness that I will never forget.

It has been 10 months now, but I can still feel the pain like I felt it that morning. Which is why I had no intentions of writing about it in this book. I did not want to re-live this experience. However, I believe the Spirit of the Lord wanted me to express how fearful, and vulnerable I was but yet 10 months later, I can write about it. Was I scared? Of course. I was terrified. I was afraid of what people would think of me. I was afraid to feel those feelings again. I was afraid that I would be judged harshly as a Professional with four degrees and numerous certifications. But nevertheless, the Father's will had to be done.

42258449R00049

Made in the USA
Middletown, DE
13 April 2019